Unraveling The Potency of Customer Relationship Management (CRM)

Nishant Baxi

ISBN 978-93-5883-097-2
© Nishant Baxi 2023

Published in India 2023 by Pencil

A brand of
One Point Six Technologies Pvt. Ltd.
Unit no. 26, Ground Floor, Building A1,
Wadala Truck Terminal Road,
Near Post Office, Antop Hill, Mumbai - 400037
E connect@thepencilapp.com
W www.thepencilapp.com

Author biography

I am an experienced content creator and digital/social media marketing professional with a demonstrated history of working in the publishing industry. I am skilled in E-Learning, Market Research, Online Advertising, Management, and Business Development, Content Development.

CONTENTS

Preface

This eBook's target audience includes budding entrepreneurs, small-to-medium business owners, and complex enterprise organizations keen on understanding how to utilize CRM to maximize profitability and productivity.

Introduction

Definition of Customer Relationship Management (CRM)
Customer relationship management (CRM) represents an integral concept employed in all business settings as an effective strategy to manage a company's interaction with its customers (1). Described as a blend of practices, strategies, and technologies, CRM seeks to improve customer service relationships and optimize customer retention, thereby increasing sales growth.

The value of CRM systems cannot be overstated. They compile customer data across different channels, or points of contact, between the customer and the company. These points of contact could be the company's website, telephone, live chat, direct mail, marketing materials, and social media. CRM systems also provide information on customers' personal information, purchase history, buying preferences, and concerns.

By collecting this detailed customer information, businesses can serve their clients better. Personalized relationships with customers can be established, with a focus on improving customer satisfaction. Consequently, the effectiveness of marketing efforts is improved, leading to enhanced profitability (2).

The implementation of CRM strategies leads to significant benefits that positively impact business operations. One evident advantage is the increase in customer retention and revenue. Since it costs more to attract new customers than to retain existing ones, businesses must make efforts to keep their current clients satisfied (3). With CRM systems, businesses can automate the routine tasks of sales, service, and marketing, freeing staff to concentrate on customer service and attracting new customers.

CRM tools also help businesses in mitigating risks and making accurate forecasts. By analyzing buying habits and customer trends, they can predict future sales trends and enable businesses to plan accordingly, avoiding costly overstocking or understocking. Furthermore, CRM can provide an early warning of potential problems, like customer dissatisfaction or falling sales, so that necessary corrective actions can be taken promptly.

Choosing a CRM system suitable for a business depends on the specific needs of the business. However, functional elements such as salesforce automation, contact, and lead management, reporting and analytics, and integration with other software are crucial when selecting a CRM system (4).

At its core, CRM is not merely about implementing a specific technology but rather a philosophy that places customers at the heart of business operations. By effectively employing CRM strategies, businesses can foster enduring relationships with their customers, leading to sustained business growth and success.

A brief explanation of the importance of CRM in businesses

Customer Relationship Management (CRM) plays a critical role in revolutionizing business processes and strategy. Regardless of the size or nature of any business, whether service-oriented or product-based, CRM forms the core that ensures customer satisfaction and retention. CRM is a powerful tool that helps businesses manage their relationships with customers and potential customers, ultimately leading to growth (Gordon, 2019).

By definition, CRM refers to the practices, principles, strategies, and technology that businesses utilize to manage and analyze customer interactions throughout their lifecycle. The primary objective of CRM is to improve business relationships, facilitate customer retention, and drive sales growth (Buttle & Maklan, 2015).

CRM's importance in business is multifaceted. Firstly, it aids in centralizing customer information and streamlining access to data for businesses. This centralized database reduces response times, helping businesses react swiftly to customer needs. Additionally, it improves staff productivity, saving valuable time that would have been otherwise spent on searching for customer information.

Another advantage lies in the enhanced communication that CRM promotes. Having a single, comprehensive customer database allows any employee, not just those involved directly in sales or customer relations, to provide quality assistance to customers. It eliminates potential confusion, effectively improving customer experience and strengthening trust (Choudhury & Harrigan, 2014).

Thirdly, CRM facilitates precise target marketing, a pivotal strategy for modern businesses seeking to attract and retain dedicated customers. Segmentation based on previous purchases, communication history, and other preferences enables personalized marketing, making customers feel uniquely valued and consequently more loyal to the brand.

Moreover, CRM's analytical capabilities can drive sales. Providing data analysis on sales trends, customer behavior, and market demand, CRM can help businesses tailor their offerings to meet clientele needs. It aids in timely decision-making, risk forecasting, and strategic planning, all crucial elements for improved financial performance (Trainor, 2012).

Lastly, CRM aids in creating a seamless sales strategy. It consolidates customer contacts, account details, lead sourcing, tracking, and processing. This provides a clear view of stages in the sales cycle and assists in opportunity recognition and conversion, leading to increased sales.

In conclusion, CRM has emerged as an indispensable business tool in this era of cut-throat competition. Successful CRM strategies lead to improved customer satisfaction, loyalty, retention, and profitable growth. However, businesses need to select CRM systems that align with their objectives and capabilities, ensuring maximum utilization.

UNDERSTANDING CRM Evolution of CRM from traditional to digital

The world of customer relationship management (CRM) has dramatically evolved over the years — from simple directories to advanced, cloud-based digital services that offer an array of functionalities.

CRM evolution began in the late 1980s with the advent of database marketing. Companies leveraged customer databases to track interactions and improve future marketing efforts (Bradford, Kreiss, Rosen, & Shafir, 2018).

Through the 1990s, companies realized that understanding customers required a broader perspective than merely transaction data. As a result, the focus shifted from transactional to relational marketing, ushering in the era of traditional CRM. These CRM systems captured wider data, including customer feedback and complaints. This era saw the rise of renowned CRM software vendors like Siebel and Salesforce, who began to dominate the market in the late 90s (Stone, Woodcock, & Wilson, 1996).

By the early 2000s, Internet technology became widespread, transforming CRM systems into web-based tools. It offered customers direct interaction with businesses online and helped in effective customer segmentation and personalized marketing. Despite these advancements, these CRM systems were still complex, expensive, and required intense IT support for execution (Peppers & Rogers, 2004).

In the late 2000s, with the advent of cloud computing, CRM experienced another extraordinary revolution. Cloud-based CRM tools like Salesforce.com (launched in 1999) and Microsoft Dynamics CRM (released in 2011) altered the CRM landscape. These digital CRM systems were far more flexible, and scalable and offered a myriad of capabilities such as social media integration and mobile access. The migration to the cloud-based system was further boosted by the availability of the Software as a Service (SaaS) model which made CRM systems affordable and feasible for small businesses (Trainor, 2012).

Presently, CRMs are revolving around big data analytics, machine learning, and artificial intelligence (AI). These cutting-edge technologies provide predictive analytics, automation, and customization that improve interaction with customers on multiple channels. Today's CRMs are more customer-centric and capable of handling complex tasks like sentiment analysis, customer churn prediction, and targeted marketing, thus helping businesses create strong customer relationships and achieve remarkable customer satisfaction (Ngai, Xiu, & Chau, 2009).

In summary, CRM systems have undergone significant transformations from being simple customer databases to becoming smarter, customer-centric, analytical, and digital tools. As technology advances further, CRM systems are set to become even more intelligent, thereby assisting businesses in managing customer relationships more efficiently and effectively.

Varieties of CRM – Operational, Analytical, and Collaborative CRM

Customer Relationship Management (CRM) has emerged as an essential instrument for managing and improving business relationships. Learning the different forms of CRM – operational, analytical, and collaborative - is necessary to understand how businesses can utilize this tool to perfect their customer interaction and service deliverance.

Firstly, operational CRM is the most common form of CRM and refers to systems that provide support for various business processes involving direct interaction with customers. This type of CRM is predominantly about automation and improvement of customer-facing and customer-centric processes like marketing, sales, and service (Levine, 2012). Operational CRM aids businesses in lead generation, conversion, and providing service and support to customers, enhancing the overall customer experience.

Analytical CRM, the second variety, relies heavily on data analysis. Unlike operational CRM, this type does not interact directly with customers. Its main focus is to gather customer data from various sources, analyze it, and use this information to enhance and personalize customer interaction (Nguyen, Sherif, & Newby, 2007). This form of CRM helps companies understand customer behaviors, determine customer value, and identify customer needs and preferences using data mining, pattern recognition, and other advanced analytics.

Lastly, the collaborative CRM mainly concentrates on communication and collaboration with customers. This type involves all the channels that customers use to communicate with the company, like email, calls, social media, etc., and works on integrating and automating these channels to provide a seamless customer experience (Greenberg, 2010). The primary goal of collaborative CRM is to ensure that every customer interaction across all touchpoints is consistent, personalized, and efficient.

In conclusion, each CRM - operational, analytical, and collaborative - contributes to creating a comprehensive and cohesive customer strategy. Operational CRM helps automate business processes involving customers, analytical CRM aids in understanding customers deeply through data analysis, and collaborative CRM focuses on enhancing communication with customers. Therefore, depending on a business's specific needs, one type or a combination of CRM types could be employed to ensure a holistic approach to improving customer relationships and enhancing customer retention.

Key components of a CRM system

Customer Relationship Management (CRM) serves as an essential tool for businesses in the modern era. CRM enables businesses to streamline their processes, maintain customer relations, increase sales, and heighten profitability. However, for a CRM system to be profitable and function optimally, it requires some key components. These components define the main structure and functionality of the system while significantly impacting its efficacy (Kumar & Reinartz, 2012).

The first key component of a CRM system is contact management. It is crucial to have a well-organized record of customers' details, including communication history and interactions with the company. With this component, a CRM system can track sales activities, conversations, deals, and other relevant customer interactions.

Secondly, a CRM system should offer a sales force automation feature. By automatically recording all stages in a sales process, the system can track each transaction. This feature enables sales teams to focus more on selling and less on the process, thereby increasing productivity.

Interaction tracking is another critical component, responsible for recording a customer's engagements and interactions with a brand. This insight allows businesses to deliver relevant, personalized marketing and service to each customer.

The fourth key component is email tracking. CRM systems should allow businesses to centrally consolidate and manage customer emails. This facilitates easy tracking of communications, maintaining a clear customer conversation history, and ensuring nothing slip through the cracks.

Additionally, social media management has become an increasingly important component of CRM systems. This feature enables businesses to engage, interact, and monitor customer behavior through social media platforms with ease (Trainor et al., 2014).

The reporting and dashboard feature is another crucial part of a CRM system. It gives businesses the capability to generate informational reports and visualize data through graphical representations. This highly valuable component offers insights to improve decision-making.

Finally, the mobile support component is very beneficial, allowing staff to access the CRM system anytime, anywhere, hence increasing efficiency and effectiveness.

In conclusion, the CRM system is more than a tool; it is the backbone of excellent customer service for many businesses as it offers several benefits to businesses. It streamlines processes, increases sales, enhances customer service, and supports the firm's overall performance. Therefore, it is crucial to understand the key components of a CRM system to enjoy maximum benefits.

THE RELEVANCE OF CRM IN BUSINESS

Improving business relationships

In today's highly competitive business environment, fostering strong, productive customer relationships is critical for success. One way businesses achieve this vital objective is through the implementation of a Customer Relationship Management (CRM) system. CRM is not just a technology; it is a strategy designed to help businesses learn more about their customers and their needs to enhance their customer relations.

CRM revolves around managing all facets of interaction that a company has with its customers, whether being sales or service-related. It helps to understand the customers' needs and behavior, thereby building a relationship with them (Greenberg, 2010). A well-executed CRM system can yield impressive benefits in enhancing a business's functionality and leading it to successive high grounds.

The relevance of CRM applications in the business environment cannot be overstated. They play a fundamental role in understanding and managing customer behavior, which is imperative in this era of tough competition. A study suggests that over 91% of businesses with more than 11 employees utilize CRM systems (Beasty, 2006). One of the advantages of using CRM in business is it helps lead to customer satisfaction, which in turn creates customer loyalty and retention, maximizing profitability.

Furthermore, CRM helps in automating numerous mundane tasks. Automation saves time for other functional departments like marketing, sales, and customer service departments, allowing them to focus on more productive tasks. It streamlines business processes, which, in return, improves operational efficiency, decreases operational costs, and raises overall profitability.

Moreover, CRM systems provide businesses with invaluable insights into customer preferences, buying habits, and engagements with the brand by collecting and organizing information across different channels. These insights make it possible for businesses to make informed business decisions, customize their offerings, provide superior customer services, and improve overall business performance.

With the advent of mobile CRM and social CRM, businesses can interact with customers in real-time, thus leading to better customer service and more robust customer relationships. These new developments in CRM are proving to be new push points for businesses in retaining customers and also acquiring new ones.

In conclusion, businesses should prioritize implementing a robust CRM system as it plays a vital role in relationship management with customers. Well-nurtured customer relationships, enhanced operational efficiency, more informed decision-making, higher customer satisfaction, and increasing profit margins are some of the benefits that reaffirm the importance and relevance of CRM in the business world.

Streamlining business operations

Unraveling The Potency of Customer Relationship Management (CRM)

In an era where the business environment is becoming increasingly competitive and customer-centric, maintaining a robust business-customer relationship is an essential element of business success. In this context, the role of Customer Relationship Management (CRM) systems becomes prominent. CRM is a strategic approach that relates to core business processes to enhance client relationships, boost sales growth, and increase overall business profitability (Nguyen, Sherif, & Newby, 2007). This chapter highlights the relevance of CRM in streamlining business operations.

CRM systems provide a centralized platform that interlinks all departments, thereby ensuring seamless communication and collaboration among the various teams. They gather data from various customer interactions and present it in a comprehensive manner that enables businesses to understand customer behavior better. This data-driven insight is crucial in making strategic decisions and implementing relevant customer-oriented policies that bolster customer loyalty and enhance sales growth (Khodakarami & Chan, 2014).

In sales management, CRM plays an instrumental role. By automating certain sales tasks, CRM systems save time and boost efficiency. Moreover, they provide real-time updates on sales metrics that help formulate effective sales strategies. Additionally, they assist in managing the sales pipeline effectively, thereby ensuring a steady flow of revenue.

Also, CRM aids significantly in the provision of excellent customer service. It equips businesses with an understanding of customer preferences, habits, and pain points, assisting in providing personalized services that lead to heightened satisfaction levels (Trainor, Andzulis, Rapp, & Agnihotri, 2014). Consequently, businesses experience an increased customer retention rate, leading to stable revenue generation.

Further, CRM acts as an effective tool for marketing. It facilitates segmentation of customers based on demographics, buying behavior, and other parameters, therefore enabling targeted marketing. It also enables tracking of campaign success and customer response, providing invaluable insights for future campaigns.

Lastly, CRM tools promote scalability. With their cloud-based systems that can accommodate an unlimited amount of information, CRM tools can facilitate growth. As businesses expand, the CRM system grows with them, always ready to handle any increased load.

In conclusion, the relevance of CRM in streamlining business operations is undeniable. CRM systems play a substantial role in enhancing internal operations, boosting sales growth, promoting efficient marketing, improving customer service, and steering business growth. Therefore, to thrive in today's competitive business environment, the adoption and effective use of CRM systems should be prioritized.

Enhancing customer service

Customer Relationship Management (CRM) should not be underestimated in today's business environment as it is an essential tool for ensuring optimal customer satisfaction and loyalty. In the rapidly evolving digital era where consumer behavior, demands, and expectations are ever-shifting, employing CRM in business practices can effectively enhance customer service.

CRM is widely recognized for its ability to catalog customer information - a critical feature when tailoring services directly to individual consumer needs. Through this profiling, businesses can better understand their customers and therefore serve them more effectively.

In an era where personalization is at the forefront of customer service, the customer profile information offered by a robust CRM assists businesses in creating individualized experiences. Companies can draw invaluable insights from this data, enabling them to deliver targeted solutions. Whether it's recommending products based on purchasing and browsing behavior or providing personalized customer support, CRM is pivotal in maintaining a positive relationship with customers (Peppers & Rogers, 2016).

Moreover, CRM systems supply businesses with customer service tools that help track, manage, and resolve issues promptly. Operational efficiency is greatly improved through the use of automatic ticket generation and prioritization, issue tracking, and effective solutions management. This means that customers' complaints, inquiries, and issues can be handled more swiftly and efficiently, consequently leading to increased customer satisfaction (Mishra, Modgil, & Kapoor, 2017).

The essence of CRM extends beyond issue resolution to include proactive communication with customers. Maintaining regular contact with customers helps businesses understand their needs, anticipate their demands, and respond effectively. CRM software facilitates this engagement through email marketing, social media management, and other customer outreach programs.

Lastly, CRM enhances business decisions with comprehensive reporting and analytics tools. By visualizing customer behavior and trends, these tools inform businesses on where improvements can be made. For instance, the software may indicate low response rates to a certain marketing tactic, encouraging alteration of the strategy. The ability of CRM to provide real-time feedback can help a business in adapting and growing according to the needs of its customers (Trainor, Andzulis, Rapp, & Agnihotri, 2014).

In conclusion, the relevance of CRM in business practices cannot be overstated. It enhances customer service by allowing for personalization, improving operational efficiency, enabling proactive communication, and supplying insightful data for decision-making. By leveraging a robust CRM system, businesses can ensure improved customer satisfaction and loyalty, resulting in sustainable growth and profitability.

Retaining existing clients and attracting new ones

In the current global business framework, where competition is tougher than ever, customer relationship management (CRM) plays a crucial role in sustaining a business. CRM refers to the principles, practices, and guidelines that successful businesses follow to interact with customers. It leverages data analysis about customers' history with a company to improve business relationships with customers, specifically focusing on customer retention and ultimately driving sales growth (Zikmund, McLeod & Gilbert, 2003).

A good CRM system provides businesses with a clear overview of their customers. These overviews can range from simple data like their contact information to more complicated data, including customer interactions, purchase history, preferences, and concerns. With this knowledge in place, businesses can efficiently target their offerings and enhance overall customer service. A well-crafted CRM strategy allows businesses to differentiate themselves from competitors by focusing on their customers.

One key aspect that CRM solutions effectively address is the relevance of focusing on long-term client management rather than short-term profitability. According to the Harvard Business Review, stopping service to a customer who is expensive to serve, doesn't pay much, or is just demanding, doesn't help much in terms of profitability. On the contrary, companies need to handle these customers properly and change them into desirable customers. This is possible with the help of an effective CRM that aims at obtaining insights about the factors that lead to customer dissatisfaction and working on them (Kumar and Reinartz, 2012).

Additionally, CRM provides the power to businesses to provide an individualized customer experience based on their buying palates, history, and preferences. With the sheer volume and the complexity of customer data today, companies are investing in technologies like CRM to convert this data into actionable insights. Personalizing the customer experience isn't just a sound business strategy, but it's also a way to build a loyal clientele.

Moreover, CRM is not just about businesses retaining their existing clients. An integrated CRM assists in bringing new customers through lead generation and customer referral programs. It helps in managing leads from the nurturing process, through the customers' various points of engagement, to conversion. The software can also monitor past sale patterns to predict future needs, leading to repeat sales (Lee, Y., Lee, J., & Lee, S. 2005).

In conclusion, the relevance of CRM in businesses today cannot be overstressed. Retaining existing clients and attracting new ones is the name of the game, and a thoughtfully implemented CRM system is an impressive asset in achieving these objectives.

Facilitating business growth and profitability.

The significance of Customer Relationship Management (CRM) in the corporate world cannot be overemphasized. CRM, as an approach, involves the management of interactions with current, potential, and past customers, focusing on improving business relationships with them to foster customer retention and drive business growth (House, 2017).

Firstly, CRM provides a systematic way of storing and managing customer information in a centralized database that can be accessed by all members of a business. Having a consolidated platform with a complete data source not only avoids the repetition of tasks but also minimizes the chances of losing valuable information. This can positively impact productivity and decision-making effectiveness, hence driving profitability (Francis & Whitefield, 2018).

Secondly, CRM enhances communication within a business setting. It allows information to be shared easily among team members, enhancing collaboration and coordination. This improved communication leads to faster response times to customer queries and higher levels of customer satisfaction, thus fostering customer retention, an essential component for business growth (Sterne, 2017). Moreover, leveraging CRM allows businesses to deliver personalized customer experiences. Thus, CRM tracks customer preferences and behavior, leveraging this information to customize products, services, and marketing efforts. Personalized experiences result in increased customer loyalty and ultimately impact business profitability positively (Stanleigh, 2019).

SELECTING A CRM SYSTEM

Determining your business needs

Choosing the correct Customer Relationship Management (CRM) system is one of the most vital business decisions that can significantly impact profit, productivity, and customer retention among other aspects.

A CRM system effectively facilitates organization and management of customer data- attracting potential customers, providing services to existing ones, and retaining old customers enhance business performance dramatically. Enhancing customer service and unwavering customer loyalty are the compelling reasons to implement a reliable CRM system.

However, understanding your specific business needs is the initial, most crucial step in the selection of the CRM. Multiple CRM systems cater to different business types, sizes, and dynamics. For instance, CRM solutions tailored for large corporate businesses may be inappropriate for small businesses due to their resource constraints. Some CRM systems are industry-specific, containing unique features suitable for certain business sectors only. Therefore, analyze your business size, industry, and general needs before choosing a CRM system.

Moreover, the CRM system must be capable of serving your specific business needs. A business looking to improve customer service will have different CRM needs than a business looking for sales force automation. For improving customer service, a CRM system capable of offering help-desk solutions, tracking customer interactions, and delivering accurate customer data would be suitable. Similarly, for a business looking for sales automation, the CRM should be capable of task automation, sales forecasting, and actionable insights.

Consider the CRM system's customizable features. Every business has unique needs; a flexible CRM system could adapt to the individual needs of a business. For instance, it should be able to support your preferred communication channels or customer contact points. CRM features like task automation, contact management, and document storage should be adjustable to the specifics of your operations.

Cost consideration is another important factor. Your preferred CRM solution should align with your budget constraints without compromising on essential features. High-cost CRM systems usually offer more advanced features but may be not feasible for small businesses. Always prioritize affordability over extra features that may not be relevant to your business needs.

Lastly, make sure to consider the user-friendliness of the CRM system. An ideal CRM system should be easy to use and understand by the staff for optimal performance. A CRM system with an intuitive user interface and easy navigation increases user adoption rates and consequently, business productivity.

Choosing the right CRM system could mean the difference between business success and failure. Thus, determining your business needs before choosing a CRM system is of paramount importance.

Features to look for in a CRM system

The search for the right Customer Relationship Management (CRM) system can be overwhelming, given the plethora of software available in the market. However, certain key features consistently stay relevant in determining the effectiveness of a CRM system. Here are the main features to look for when choosing a CRM system for your business.

1. Contact Management:

The primary feature of any CRM is to adequately manage contacts. This encompasses storing contact details, tracking interactions, and classifying customers based on preferences or past interactions. An ideal CRM should serve as a comprehensive database for customer information (1).

2. Interaction tracking:

A CRM should track every interaction with a customer such as emails, phone calls, meetings, and messages across all channels. This helps in maintaining a consistent tone in communication and facilitates personalized marketing strategies (2).

3. Task Management.

The ability to assign, track, and manage tasks is crucial for a CRM system. From scheduling meetings to closing sales, an effective CRM platform should keep track of every task and deadline involved in the customer journey (3).

4. Sales Forecasting:

Another feature to look for is sales forecasting, which uses historical data to predict future sales trends. This feature helps managers to make informed business decisions and plan resources (4).

5. Integration:

The ability to integrate with other business applications is a significant plus. An ideal CRM should integrate seamlessly with email systems, calendar apps, and ERP systems, enabling sharing and synchronization of data among all platforms (5).

6. Mobility:

In today's fast-paced business environment, having access to CRM from anywhere is essential. A CRM mobile app can help sales teams update customer information on the go.

7. Customization:

Every business is different and needs different solutions. A good CRM system offers customizable features to suit specific business needs (6).

8. User-Friendly Interface:

An intuitive and user-friendly interface is a must. It decreases the training time and ensures rapid adoption among the team.

9. Security:

Given that a CRM system handles sensitive customer data, it is crucial to ensure the safety and integrity of the data. Security features like data encryption, user authentication, and access controls are necessary to prevent data breaches (7).

10. Customer Support:

Robust customer support can make or break a CRM experience. The CRM system you select must offer various support options like email, phone, and chat (8).

Selecting the right CRM system will always depend on your specific business needs. The features listed above are some of the most common ones to look for when choosing a

CRM.

Comparison of leading CRM systems in the market – pros and cons, costs, user reviews

As businesses scale and diversify, Customer Relationship Management (CRM) systems have become an indispensable tool. These systems streamline the entire marketing process by organizing customer data, enhancing interactions with clients, and boosting profitability. This chapter presents a comparison of three leading CRM systems in the market - Salesforce, Zoho, and Microsoft Dynamics, focusing on their pros, cons, costs, and user reviews.

Salesforce, the dominant player in the CRM market, is lauded for its comprehensive and robust system (Gartner, 2020). It offers an extensive array of attributes including sales forecasting, collaboration, analytics and automation, email marketing, and customer service. Salesforce is praised for its user-friendly interface and its ever-evolving functionalities. However, the system's main drawbacks include high costs and complexity, which make it less ideal for small businesses (PCMag, 2019). A Salesforce license ranges from $25 per user/month for the Essentials package to $300 per user/month for the Unlimited package. Its review score on G2 stands at 4.2 out of 5.

Zoho CRM, on the other hand, is celebrated for its affordability and simplicity (TechRadar, 2021). Offering features such as lead management, sales force automation, and customer support, Zoho is ideal for small- to mid-sized businesses. The primary criticism of Zoho is its limited customization capabilities compared to its competitors. Zoho's price tag ranges from free for its basic package, to $100 per user/month for the Ultimate package.

Its G2 review score is 3.9 out of 5.

Microsoft Dynamics, a comprehensive CRM tool, excels in its deep integration with other Microsoft products, making it a preferred choice for businesses already using a Microsoft ecosystem (Capterra, 2020). Dynamics provides features including sales force automation, customer support, and marketing automation. However, its steep learning curve and occasional glitches work against it. Dynamics CRM pricing starts at $65 per user/month for the professional package to $210 for the advanced package. Its review score on G2 is 3.9 out of 5.

In summary, the 'best' CRM is dependent on a business's specific needs and resources. While Salesforce's expansive features and robustness make it the standard for larger corporations, Zoho's affordability and simplicity are ideal for smaller businesses. Meanwhile, businesses already operating within a Microsoft ecosystem might find Dynamics CRM a seamless addition.

All three CRM systems have their unique strengths and weaknesses. Consequently, businesses are encouraged to thoroughly analyze their options by considering costs, operational requirements, scalability, user reviews, and most importantly, the CRM's ability to address the business's specific pain points and objectives.

CRM also allows for improved segmentation of customers. By categorizing customers based on their behaviors and preferences, businesses can target their marketing strategies more effectively. The meticulous targeting of CRM results in more sales, increased revenue, and ultimately, profitability (Thomas, 2019).

Finally, CRM facilitates better post-sales service. It enables businesses to track customer issues and complaints, ensuring they are addressed promptly. This leads to better customer satisfaction, strengthening the relationship between the business and its customers, which is vital for customer retention and business growth (Sterne, 2017).

In conclusion, CRM is a crucial tool for businesses striving for sustained growth and profitability. By facilitating efficient data management, improved communication, personalized customer experiences, effective customer segmentation, and superior post-sales service, CRM plays a vital role in fostering customer satisfaction and retention; elements critical to business success.

Steps to implement CRM in an organization

In the current digital business environment, managing customer relationships is paramount. CRM is a strategic framework that organizations employ to understand customers' needs, manage and analyze interactions, and improve business relationships. Now, let's dissect the implementation steps for CRM in any organization.

Step 1: Define CRM Goals

The first step entails specifying the objectives of implementing the CRM. This is based on the needs, challenges, and strategic directions of the organization. Goals can range from customer retention, increasing sales, or improving customer service (Grant, 2014).

Step 2: Form a CRM Project Team

Effective CRM project teams consist of qualified personnel from relevant departments such as sales, IT, customer service, and marketing. This team will steer the implementation process.

Step 3: Identify Customer Needs

Understanding the needs of customers forms a cornerstone in CRM. Organizations must take a customer-oriented perspective towards meeting customer expectations.

Step 4: Select CRM Provider & Software

Another crucial step is selecting the right CRM software and provider that matches the business requirements. Options should be evaluated based on cost, compatibility, customization capability, and ease of use (Trainor et al., 2014).

Step 5: Customize the CRM Solution

Some CRM software may require customization to align with the unique needs of the organization. For instance, the sale process may be tweaked, or new data fields added.

Step 6: Train the Users

Training is essential to ensure that employees familiarize themselves with the new system. The training should cover all the primary functions of the CRM and continual support must be provided.

Step 7: Deploy the CRM System

The CRM is then launched, ensuring all functions and features are working as requisite. Feedback during this rollout will help to troubleshoot and streamline system usage.

Step 8: Monitor and Evaluate the CRM Performance

After deploying the CRM system, its performance should be regularly monitored, and its impact on the organization evaluated. Tracking tools like KPIs can be used to measure the success rate.

In conclusion, implementing CRM in an organization is a strategic choice that can foster customer satisfaction, organizational efficiency, and competitive advantage. An effective CRM implementation not only helps manage customer relationships but also uncovers vital insights for data-driven decision-making. Careful planning and execution of the steps mentioned above can ensure a successful CRM rollout.

EFFECTIVE STRATEGIES FOR MANAGING A CRM SYSTEM

Role of management in successful CRM adoption

A strong customer relationship management (CRM) system is a cornerstone of successful businesses in just about every industry. Yet, simply investing in CRM software isn't enough to automatically mint success. Indeed, effective CRM integration and use largely hinge on the establishment of company culture and operational processes to support the CRM strategy, all of which begins with management.

Management plays a pivotal role in the adoption and successful execution of CRM systems. Effective leadership is often the defining factor between CRM failure and success (Kim et al., 2012). Here's how:

1. Establishing & Communicating CRM Strategy

Management is responsible for setting the CRM strategy, defining its goals, and communicating the same throughout the organization. Clear communication of objectives and expectations helps secure buy-in from all staff, ensuring collective effort towards a shared goal (Rigby et al., 2002).

2. Staff Training

The successful adoption of CRM systems requires aptly trained personnel. Managers should organize relevant

CRM systems training to enhance employee understanding and efficient use. Regular refresher courses are also vital to keep pace with upgrades and mitigate skill fade – again, this falls under management's purview (Chen & Popovich, 2003).

3. Management Involvement

Management's active involvement encourages employees to use the CRM system effectively. Certainly, seeing senior executives utilizing CRM sends a powerful message. It shows that CRM isn't simply a tool for junior employees, but a strategy that drives the entire business (Trainor et al., 2014).

4. User Support

Very often, after the initial setup and training, staff may face challenges when using a CRM system. Supportive management can help address these issues timely and effectively, thereby making the adoption process smoother (Mendoza et al., 2007).

5. Change Management

The introduction of CRM systems invariably calls for change. Management plays a key role in managing the change process, mitigating resistance, and ensuring a smooth transition. This includes revising processes, roles, and performance metrics to align with the CRM strategy.

6. Evaluation and Continuous Refinement

Management must continuously evaluate the effectiveness of the CRM system and refine strategies as necessary. This requires performance metrics that align with CRM goals and regular analysis of the data generated by the CRM (Pedron & Saccol, 2009).

The role of management is crucial in the successful adoption of a CRM system, acting as the linchpin that holds together all elements of a successful CRM strategy. While the CRM system provides the tools, it is sound management that truly drives CRM success.

Training staff for CRM implementation

Effective CRM implementation demands more than merely purchasing the right software. It requires the readiness and proper training of staff to use and optimize the system efficiently. According to a Forrester Research report, 47% of all CRM initiatives fail, primarily because of inadequate employee training (Forrester Research, 2018). This chapter will explore the importance of staff training and how organizations can successfully implement CRM.

The CRM is a tool meant to enhance customer service, track interactions, manage contacts, improve client relationships, and drive sales. A CRM system is only as good as the team members utilizing it. Staff training, therefore, is not an option but an imperative step in the CRM implementation process.

Training ensures that staff are equipped with the necessary knowledge and skills to utilize the CRM to its full potential (Salesforce, 2019). User adoption of the system is also positively correlated with adequate training. They feel more comfortable and confident using the tool when they understand it well, leading to a higher return on investment.

To achieve effective CRM training, the first step is to analyze and understand the current skill level of employees. This analysis helps to develop a training plan catered to their needs.

Next is crafting the training material. Make it as practical and relatable as possible. Using actual scenarios that the staff is likely to encounter in their work environment would be helpful. Introducing the staff to real-use cases can help them comprehend how the CRM will simplify their tasks and improve productivity (CRM Switch, 2017).

A systematic training approach is also essential. This could involve initial briefing sessions, hands-on practical sessions, and a follow-up. Employees should not only know the 'how' but also the 'why' of using the system.

Also, consider employing a variety of training methods, including in-person training sessions, webinars, video tutorials, and one-on-one coaching. This allows the employees to choose the training method that suits them best while ensuring all get properly trained on the system (BDC, 2019).

Remember also, the importance of continuous training. CRM systems often get updated with newer features and functions and keeping the staff up-to-date with these changes is important. Encourage a culture of continuous learning and improvement.

In conclusion, quality CRM implementation is significantly dependent on staff training, centered on the needs of the employees, and should involve practical and systematic training options. Remember, a CRM system is merely a tool; the real value lies in how your team uses it.

Regularly updating and cleaning up your CRM system

Customer Relationship Management (CRM) systems play an essential role in successful businesses, especially in terms of keeping track of customer information and enhancing overall customer experience. Generally, this system integrates customer data from multiple channels, providing a centralized and accessible platform for business operations (Rouse, 2018). However, this enormous quantity of data necessitates regular updating and cleaning—also known as CRM data cleansing—to maintain the system's efficiency and accuracy.

Regular CRM system updates guarantee that the system works within the latest guidelines and maintains the best security measures in place to protect from potential cyber threats (Parker, 2019). Up-to-date software has fewer vulnerabilities and is tougher for potential cybercriminals to infiltrate. Besides, frequent updates offer access to new features and capabilities for improved performance that are often integrated to make the system more user-friendly and functional.

Data cleaning of your CRM system is equally crucial. When your system stores stale, duplicate, or inaccurate data, it compromises its effectiveness. Incorrect data can seriously impair sales performance and disrupt marketing campaigns; outdated contacts are a waste of time and resources; while duplicate data entry can obscure actual sales performance (Keene, 2017). Regular data cleansing ensures the content in the system is reliable, relevant, and useful, leading to improved decision-making in the business.

Cleaning up the CRM system also enhances data quality, which is directly related to customer satisfaction levels (Nguyen, 2020). High-quality data provides more accurate insights into customer preferences and behavior, facilitating personalized marketing strategies for better customer engagement.

While updating and cleaning the CRM system could seem like a time-consuming process, the benefits manifest in increased productivity, more accurate forecasting, and improved customer relationships (Paton, 2019). Investing time in periodic system checks not only removes stagnant data but ensures your business stays in line with evolving market trends.

Businesses must thus imbue the culture of regular CRM updating and cleaning as an organizational best practice. It ensures the data consistently aligns with the real-life customer base. This way, businesses can maintain the customer database's relevance and maximize the potential benefits from their CRM systems.

In conclusion, a well-maintained CRM system is a crucial asset for successful businesses. In the age of data-driven decisions, maintaining the accuracy and reliability of this data should be a priority. Therefore, regularly updating and cleaning your CRM system should be part of your business's routine.

Monitoring and evaluation of CRM practices

Customer Relationship Management (CRM) has emerged as an integral business strategy for all industries. Implementing CRM practices is just one part of the equation. Businesses need to be keen on monitoring and evaluating these practices to ensure their efficacy in achieving business objectives (Tan & Sousa, 2015).

CRM practices involve identifying customer requirements, personalizing customer interactions, and developing strategies aimed at enhancing customer satisfaction and loyalty. The focus is on managing an employer-business relationship that benefits both the organization and the customer (Nguyen, Sherif, & Newby, 2007). Monitoring and evaluating CRM practices should be an ongoing process to ensure that the practices remain adaptive to changing business and customer needs.

Monitoring involves tracking the operations of CRM practices. It entails the regular checking and recording of activities to assess their performance against a set plan or standards. Various tools can be used for the real-time monitoring of CRM practices. Tools that provide data visualization, predictive analytics, and real-time reporting are essential (Chen & Popovich, 2003). Monitoring hence goes beyond merely tracking the number of customer interactions but provides deep insights into each interaction's quality and impact.

Monitoring CRM practices helps determine if a business is on the right track towards achieving its predetermined objectives. It allows for timely identification and resolution of potential problems, minimizing any negative impact on the overall business performance (Chen & Popovich, 2003).

Evaluation, on the other hand, offers a more comprehensive assessment of the CRM practices. It involves gauging the effectiveness and efficiency of these methods in meeting the pre-set business objectives. Factors assessed in the evaluation process include the level of customer satisfaction, customer retention rates, and revenue growth. Frequent customer surveys and collecting feedback are some of the methods used in this process (Nguyen, Sherif & Newby, 2007).

Evaluating CRM practices allows a business to quash ineffective strategies, amplify successful ones, and explore new opportunities. It also helps to ensure that CRM strategies align with the overarching business strategy and contribute tangibly to the organization's success (Tan & Sousa, 2015).

Proper monitoring and evaluation of CRM practices contribute to the continuous improvement of strategies, enabling businesses to stay ahead in today's competitive environment. This process improves decision-making, enhances operational efficiency, and leads to a higher level of customer satisfaction.

In conclusion, CRM practices are crucial for business success. Nevertheless, the benefits can only be maximized if there is active monitoring and evaluation of these practices. Therefore, businesses should remain proactive in assessing the performance of their CRM practices to ensure they contribute positively to overall business success.

INTEGRATING CRM WITH OTHER BUSINESS SYSTEMS

The role of CRM in sales and marketing campaigns

Customer Relationship Management (CRM) is a technological tool designed to manage all your company's relationships and interactions with customers and potential customers. The ultimate goal is simple: Improve business relationships to retain existing customers and increase sales. With this in mind, CRM has a significant role in sales and marketing campaigns. Despite its diverse applications, the focus here will be on its influence on sales and marketing.

The greatest strength of a CRM system is its ability to store customer data. It acts as a database where all interactions with customers are logged, making it easier to track and analyze behavior. This data proves invaluable when planning marketing initiatives. With the ability to segment customers based on their behavior, preferences, or past interactions, targeted marketing becomes feasible (1). This leads to personalized, relevant marketing campaigns that are more likely to succeed.

From a sales perspective, CRM allows sales teams to monitor their interactions with customers, track their sales processes, measure their performance, and manage their pipeline. It provides an array of tools to automate specific tasks, thus increasing efficiency. For instance, lead management features can automatically convert marketing-qualified leads into sales-qualified leads (2). Advanced CRM systems also have prediction capabilities to deliver projections of sales trends.

CRM's role is not limited to planning and initiating marketing and sales efforts. It also aids in assessing the success of campaigns and determining Return on Investment (ROI). By tracking responses, clicks, and conversions, a CRM system can provide a clear picture of what's working and what isn't in a campaign (3).

Moreover, the integration of CRM and analytics can bring a new dimension to customer understanding. It can help firms analyze patterns in customer behavior, predict future behavior, and develop strategies off those predictions. This can, in turn, help companies sell smarter and faster while maintaining strong, sustainable customer relationships.

In the age of digital marketing, CRM becomes more essential. It helps coordinate all digital marketing efforts, including content marketing, SEO, email marketing, social media marketing, and more. This makes the campaign process more cohesive and effective, giving companies an edge in the competitive digital landscape.

Indeed, so much more can be said about the role of CRM in sales and marketing. However, at its core, CRM is about enhancing the quality of customer relationships, leading to greater customer loyalty and business success.

Integrating CRM with HR, finance, and other business software

Customer Relationship Management (CRM) software has become an indispensable tool in modern business operations as it centralizes customer data and interactions, making it easier for businesses to align their strategies and objectives with their customers' needs(1). However, to optimize businesses' operational efficiency and output, CRM integration with other organizational functions such as human resources (HR), finance, and other business software is essential.

CRM integration with HR systems not only improves internal communication but also fosters a more synergized approach towards achieving organizational goals. When HR information is combined with CRM, insights about employee performance can be linked to customer satisfaction ratings, creating a clearer understanding of how the actions of individual employees influence customer relationships(2). For instance, high-performing employees can be identified and incentivized based on the positive impact they have on customer satisfaction.

In a financial context, integrating CRM software with finance software provides a comprehensive overview of the customer's financial transactions and interactions with the business(3). By integrating these systems, businesses can employ more targeted strategies, such as segmented marketing, by analyzing customers' purchasing patterns and financial behaviors. Furthermore, integrating CRM with finance tools can aid in managing customer invoices, handling payments, and optimizing overall cash flow in the organization.

In addition, CRM software can also integrate with other business software such as Enterprise Resource Planning (ERP) systems, providing a seamless flow of information between different business functions. This integration leads to a myriad of benefits, including better decision-making, increased productivity, and enhanced customer service as all pertinent information is stored in a unified system accessible to all relevant departments(4).

To realize these benefits, organizations need to implement effective strategies and practices for CRM integration. Some key practices include defining clear integration objectives, maintaining a continuous communication flow among departments, setting proper integration processes, and rigorously testing the integrated system to ensure it functions optimally(5). Moreover, businesses can leverage professional IT service providers for seamless integration and continuous system support.

In conclusion, integrating CRM software with HR, finance, and other business software can streamline operations, thereby enhancing productivity and profitability. Enhanced information flow expedites decision-making processes, improves customer relations, and gives a competitive edge to businesses in the increasingly digital commercial landscape. Thus, businesses must consider CRM integration as a strategic move to drive organizational success in today's data-driven world.

Using CRM for business analytics.

In today's economically competitive environment, businesses must strive to effectively cater to customer needs and preferences, to ensure customer retention and amplify profits. This is where the concept of Customer Relationship Management (CRM) comes into play. CRM is a strategy designed to manage and nurture a company's relationships and interactions with potential and established customers (Salesforce, n.d.). More recently, businesses have been leveraging CRM systems not just for customer management but also for insightful business analytics.

The utility of CRM goes beyond simple customer management, it can also be used as a potent tool for business analytics. CRM systems can collect and manage massive volumes of data generated from customer interactions, and convert this data into meaningful, actionable insights. Hence, CRM has emerged as an integral tool for businesses looking to harness the power of Big Data for business analytics.

The effectiveness of CRM in business analytics can be viewed from several perspectives. Firstly, CRM systems can effectively segment customers into various categories based on numerous factors such as their purchasing behavior, preferences, and requirements, among others. This segmentation assists in the targeted marketing of products and services to consumers based on their specified categories (Morgan, 2019).

Secondly, CRM systems incorporate predictive analytics capabilities, which can predict future customer behaviors and trends based on analysis of past data. This allows businesses to anticipate customer needs, establish more successful marketing strategies, and enhance overall customer satisfaction (Morgan, 2019).

Furthermore, CRM systems permit real-time analytics, enabling businesses to make data-driven decisions promptly. With the CRM software's ability to present organized, real-time data, businesses can act upon, alter, or create marketing strategies instantaneously to receive maximum campaign effectiveness.

Alongside this, CRM analytics can also foster increased sales productivity. The data can help identify lucrative opportunities, discerning promising leads from those that are less likely to convert. This prevents wastage of time and effort, thereby enhancing the overall sales productivity (Salesforce, n.d.).

Lastly, CRM systems facilitate a unified view of a customer, gathering data from various touchpoints into a single platform. This facilitates an improved level of customer understanding, allowing businesses to tailor their offerings more accurately and build on the customer relationship (Zoho, 2021).

In conclusion, CRM systems serve as an effective instrument for business analytics, providing businesses with the necessary tools to analyze customer data and derive valuable insights. This translates into heightened sales, improved customer service, and ultimately, a stronger business.

CASE STUDIES OF SUCCESSFUL CRM IMPLEMENTATION

Industry-specific case studies highlighting the successful use of CRM

Customer Relationship Management (CRM) solutions have been utilized incredibly efficaciously across various industries, contributing to notable progress in customer-related activities. This chapter provides a vantage view through case studies on the successful integration and application of CRM in different industries.

First, let's turn our attention to the automobile industry. Volkswagen, being a leading global car manufacturer, sought to improve its customer relationships through personalized experiences. As a result, they implemented Microsoft Dynamics CRM to help streamline their businesses in over 100 countries. Interestingly, Volkswagen achieved a significant 10% surge in productivity in sales and distribution, courtesy of the smooth information flow enabled by the CRM (Microsoft, 2015).

Moving onto the healthcare industry, a sector notorious for its complex and crucial processes, CRM adoption has proven beneficial. The Nemours Children's Health System case study exemplifies this. To streamline patient service, the system integrated Salesforce CRM, which resulted in real-time virtual assistance, timely and improved patient-doctor communications, and overall improved customer satisfaction (Salesforce, 2019).

Third, in the banking sector, the Royal Bank of Scotland provides a classic example of how CRM can maximize customer satisfaction while effectively managing risks. RBS utilized Pega CRM to connect 50,000 employees across the globe, streamline the customer experience, and improve customer engagement, capturing over 95% of customer complaints instantly (Pega, 2017).

In the e-commerce domain, giants like Amazon efficiently use CRM. To understand and target customer needs, Amazon uses a data-driven approach, using data-fed CRMs. The CRM provides a comprehensive view of each customer, contributing to impressive service personalization and improved customer retention (Stevens, 2019).

Lastly, in the telecom industry, Verizon demonstrated how CRM can be pivotal in customer management and service enhancement. The company adopted Microsoft Dynamics 365 in a move to deliver personalized content, subsequently impacting customer engagement positively (Microsoft, 2019).

Each of these case studies shows how CRM adoption across various industries leads to impressive service personalization, improved customer retention, effective management of risks, and overall customer satisfaction.

In conclusion, CRM implementation across industries represents a paradigm shift from traditional manual operations to digital transformation. The automobile, healthcare, banking, e-commerce, and telecom industries demonstrate successful CRM adoption, proving CRM solution's universal adaptability and a promising tool for achieving customer management excellence.

Lessons learned – what worked and what did not?

Customer Relationship Management (CRM) can revolutionize a company by enhancing customer service, boosting sales, and improving a company's overall efficiency. However, successful CRM implementation requires commitment and strategic planning. Let's explore some case studies of successful CRM implementations and learn about what worked and what didn't.

1. TESCO

One of the world's leading retailers, Tesco, effectively implemented CRM to boost their customer retention rate. Tesco used data from their "Clubcard" loyalty scheme to uncover insights about shopping habits and customize their marketing efforts accordingly. By doing so, they managed to not just retain customers but procure more commitment from them.

However, their direct mail strategy didn't work as effectively due to its one-size-fits-all approach. Customers didn't respond well to generalized communication, indicating that personalization is key in CRM efforts.

2. AMAZON

E-commerce giant Amazon has become a standard-bearer for CRM. Amazon uses a recommendation system— "customers who bought this also bought..."—which has boosted up-selling and cross-selling significantly, proving the power of personalized marketing.

However, Amazon's reliance on algorithmic recommendations has occasionally misfired, offering irrelevant suggestions to customers. This points out that while technology is valuable in CRM, the human touch remains irreplaceable.

3. STARBUCKS

Starbucks has taken CRM to another level with its mobile app. The Starbucks app integrates ordering, payment, and loyalty rewards, making it a one-stop solution for customers. This strategy has significantly increased customer loyalty and overall sales.

But, Starbucks faced backlash in 2016 when they changed their rewards system, suggesting that changes to CRM systems should be made with careful consideration of customer feedback.

4. MICROSOFT

Microsoft excelled in CRM by integrating its products with LinkedIn after acquiring it. With better access to LinkedIn's professional network, Microsoft could implement a dynamic CRM ensuring details of every contact or company were updated in real-time.

However, Microsoft's one significant loss was the initial non-user-friendly interface of their CRM, which raised concerns about user experience, stressing the importance of easy-to-use CRM interfaces.

Lessons from these implementations suggest that successful CRM is about personalization, maintaining a balance between technology and the human touch, considering user experience, and most importantly, listening to customer feedback.

While CRM can greatly benefit a business, it must be carefully planned and strategically implemented. Companies must remember that CRM is not just about the technology, but about people—both your customers and your employees. Thus, CRM strategy must be customer-focused, while simultaneously making sure it assists employees in their work.

In conclusion, successful CRM implementation can be a game-changer for a company. However, it is a delicate process and must be managed carefully and strategically, keeping the customer at the center of it all.

Relevance of the case study to your business

Customer Relationship Management (CRM) systems have become a vital tool for businesses globally. They facilitate customer engagement, data collection, and analysis, and assist in the development of strategies that promote business growth. This chapter presents notable case studies of successful CRM implementation and draws out their relevance to your business.

We begin with the popular ride-hailing app, Uber. In a bid to improve its communication with customers, Uber integrated Salesforce CRM software. This adoption helped Uber streamline its customer service by enabling better tracking of customer issues and correlating them to specific trips. The results were remarkable, showing a significant decline in customer complaints (Govindarajan & Trimble, 2020). This case shows that CRM can drastically enhance customer service, thus raising customer satisfaction levels.

Next, we look at Amazon, a consistent leader in customer service. The secret to their success lies in their effective use of CRM. Amazon's CRM collects data for each customer, providing a personalized experience that increases customer loyalty. Additionally, it uses predictive analytics to suggest products, contributing to increased sales (Pani, 2017). This case is a clear illustration that CRM systems can promote personalized experiences, leading to not only customer retention but also sales growth.

Bancolombia, one of the largest banks in Colombia, provides an excellent example of how CRM can revolutionize business decision-making. Bancolombia implemented a CRM system that linked bank data to geospatial aspects. This innovation allowed the bank to evaluate customer creditworthiness based on both financial and geographical information. Consequently, the bank improved its understanding of its clients and the risks associated with offering them loans (Martin, 2020). This case emphasizes that CRM systems can lead to insightful decision-making that mitigates business risks.

Bosch, the global engineering and technology services company, also demonstrates a successful CRM implementation experience. Bosch adopted the SAP CRM system, which enabled effective coordination of processes across different regions and divisions, thus boosting productivity and sales revenues (SAP, n.d.). This case suggests that CRM systems, particularly when integrated company-wide, can enhance productivity and revenue.

Overall, these case studies reflect the diverse potential benefits of CRM implementation, ranging from improved customer service and personalized customer experiences to insightful decision-making and increased productivity and revenue. It's clear that any business, regardless of size or industry, can extract value from a well-implemented CRM system.

CHALLENGES AND PITFALLS IN ADOPTING CRM

Common mistakes businesses make when adopting a CRM system

Customer Relationship Management (CRM) systems are integral tools for businesses seeking to streamline customer interactions, enhance sales strategies, and improve overall business productivity. Yet, despite the high prevalence and potential benefits of CRM solutions, various pitfalls and missteps prevent businesses from fully leveraging these tools. This article aims to shine a light on common mistakes businesses make when adopting a CRM system, hoping to guide current and future adopters on a more successful path.

The first common mistake lies in the lack of clearly defined objectives (Kumar & Reinartz, 2012). Some companies plunge into the implementation phase without thoroughly grasping the system's intended purpose. They lose sight of their business's unique needs and end up with a CRM system that isn't tailored to their processes. Businesses need to start by outlining their sales, marketing, and service objectives, then select a CRM system that helps to meet those specific goals.

Secondly, companies often underestimate the significance of user training. Implementing a CRM system involves more than just software installation. It includes the employees' ability to use the software efficiently. When employees face difficulties using the CRM, they refrain from using it altogether, leading to wasted resources and unmet targets (Chen & Popovich, 2003). To avoid this, businesses should provide comprehensive training to all users, making them comfortable with the new system.

Another blunder is neglecting data quality. High-quality data is crucial for the CRM system to function optimally. If the data entered is incorrect, incomplete, or outdated, you can't expect your CRM system to yield accurate results (Eckerson, 2002). Therefore, businesses need to enforce stringent data quality controls to ensure their CRM system is fed with reliable information.

Lastly, organizations make the mistake of not reviewing and tweaking the CRM system post-implementation. It's critical to monitor the system continually, collect user feedback, and make the necessary modifications to ensure it's serving the intended purpose. Failure to do so could result in long-term failure of the CRM adoption (King & Burgess, 2008).

In conclusion, a CRM system can be a game-changer for any business if implemented correctly and utilized efficiently. Avoiding the common pitfalls listed above can pave the way for businesses to get the most out of their CRM system – improving customer relationships, driving sales, and enhancing business productivity.

How to overcome these challenges and pitfalls

Every organization seeks to improve customer relationships, streamline operations, and increase profitability. Many find a potential solution in adopting a customer relationship management (CRM) system.

However, implementing a CRM is not without its challenges and pitfalls. To ensure successful adoption and maximize the benefits, these obstacles must be overcome.

One critical challenge is ensuring efficient data migration. CRM systems rely on vast amounts of data, which needs to be cleaned, standardized, and accurately transferred to the new system. Insufficient or incorrect data can lead to inefficiencies and poor decision-making. Therefore, it is crucial to clean your data before migrating it to a new CRM system and schedule regular data clean-ups even after (Davies, 2016).

Poor user adoption is another common pitfall. CRM systems require users to change their typical workflow, which can result in resistance. Training and support are critical for overcoming this hurdle. Moreover, organization leaders should communicate the benefits of the CRM and how it simplifies work, thus encouraging user buy-in. Proper training ensures that the employees can use the system effectively, maximizing its value and improving productivity (Rouse, 2020).

Additionally, issues may arise due to a lack of integration with existing systems. Disparate systems result in data silos, making it difficult to get a unified view of customers. Overcome this by ensuring your CRM is interoperable with other systems or choosing a CRM that offers robust integration capabilities (Paul, 2019).

Choosing the right CRM system is paramount. Companies can fall into the trap of choosing a system based on cost rather than suitability to their needs. To avoid this, they should comprehensively analyze their requirements and consider factors like scalability, customization capabilities, and support service before investing in a CRM system.

Lastly, without strategic planning and management commitment, CRM adoption may not yield the desired results. It's not just about choosing the right software; leaders must align the CRM strategy with the organization's overall objectives. Leadership should actively support the project, which includes allocating sufficient resources, setting clear goals, and facilitating continuous improvement (Paul, 2019).

Overcoming these challenges is certainly not easy, but with proper planning and support, organizations can successfully adopt a CRM system, leading to improved customer relationships, operational efficiencies, and profit growth.

The future of CRM – upcoming trends and innovations

Over the past decade, Customer Relationship Management (CRM) has dramatically revolutionized how businesses interact with their customers. With the rapid advances in technology, the CRM industry is poised for significant changes. This article delves into the future of CRM and explores the upcoming trends and innovations.

CRM is moving towards further integration, with businesses expected to break down silos and share data across departments for a more cohesive customer experience. As highlighted by Gartner's 2020 report (1), by 2023, 65% of the world's organizations will have integrated their various CRM processes into a seamless system. This will allow for more streamlined operations and data-driven decision-making.

Another rising trend in CRM is the increasing reliance on artificial intelligence (AI) and machine learning (ML). AI and ML can automate repetitive tasks, provide insights from vast amounts of data, and improve customer interactions. According to Salesforce's 3rd Edition State of Service report (2), 77% of service agents in global companies declare that AI will completely transform their jobs over the next five years.

Also noteworthy is the increased use of predictive analytics in CRM. More organizations are keen to utilize data-driven insights to anticipate customer behaviors and needs. As per the statistics by Markets and Markets (3), the predictive analytics market is set to grow to $10.95 billion by 2022, indicating a growing incorporation in CRM systems.

The use of mobile CRM is on the rise too. With the ubiquity of smartphones, organizations are gravitating towards mobile CRM as it enables them to interact with customers anytime, anywhere. Nucleus Research predicts that mobile CRM will boost sales productivity by 15% (4).

Additionally, social CRM is set to shape the future of customer engagement. More businesses are opting to engage with customers through social media and are integrating CRM with social platforms for optimum efficiency. Salesforce reports that over 70% of businesses fully integrate social channels into their CRM system, marking the significance of social CRM (5).

A paramount shift in CRM is the introduction of Voice-activated CRMs. While in its infancy stages, businesses can look forward to using voice technology to engage with their CRM systems in the future. A report by OC&C Strategy Consultants states that by 2023, the voice shopping market could reach $40 billion in the US alone, influencing CRM tools to incorporate voice technology (6).

In conclusion, the future of CRM holds promising innovations that will revolutionize how businesses interact with and understand their customers. By harnessing the power of integration, AI, predictive analytics, mobile, social media, and voice-activated technology, businesses will be better placed to enhance their customer experience.

CONCLUSION

Recap of key points discussed in the eBook

The importance and strategic placement of Customer Relationship Management (CRM) in the business landscape can never be overemphasized. The in-depth coverage presented in the eBook has delineated the striking significance of CRM and its vital role in consolidating customer trust and loyalty while enhancing overall business performance.

As discussed in the eBook, CRM serves as a pivotal tool in the collection and harmonization of customer data from diverse platforms, facilitating more personalized and targeted service delivery, and forms a central part of a company's marketing strategy (Chen & Popovich, 2003). During interactions with customers, whether online or offline, all data points are aggregated and utilized in identifying customer preferences which, in turn, are instrumental in proffering tailored solutions.

A novel talking point of the eBook is the argument that, beyond its data collation capabilities, CRM has the potential to significantly boost customer satisfaction and loyalty thereby significantly improving return on investment. This is due to its emphasis on establishing and nurturing valuable and long-term customer relationships as opposed to focusing solely on sales promotion (Zablah,

Bellenger, & Johnston, 2004).

An integrative review of the eBook announces the profound relevance of CRM in the strategic planning process and managerial decision-making. Through the instrumental role CRM plays in providing reasoned customer insight, it equips management with salient information for informed decisions. Enhanced decision-making capabilities can not only optimize sales and marketing strategies but also contribute to increased competitive advantage (Chen & Popovich, 2003).

Additionally, the eBook points out that adopting CRM empowers businesses to endeavor innovative customer engagement strategies. By leveraging the analytical capabilities of CRM, businesses can effectively engage with their customer base in a more personalized and engaging manner.

The potency of CRM further lies in its ability to provide a 360-degree view of customers, allowing for more effective predictive analytics and a proactive approach to service delivery. Through this, businesses can anticipate and adequately prepare for probable changes in customer behavior, thus operating a step ahead of their competition (Zablah, Bellenger, & Johnston, 2004).

In conclusion, the in-depth discussion in the eBook spotlights the integral role of CRM in business operations. It is not just a tool but a strategic asset, promoting customer satisfaction and loyalty, thereby enhancing overall business performance.

From the insights gleaned from this eBook, any company, regardless of its scale, can leverage CRM's potential to drive customer-focused marketing and service delivery strategies.

Final thoughts on the importance and implementation of an effective CRM system for businesses

Customer Relationship Management system, known as CRM, is not purely a technology but more so a business strategy. In the current fast-paced digital era where customers are the lifeblood of any business, a reliable and effective CRM system is profoundly significant. This article applauds CRM's effectiveness and further analyzes its implementation.

The importance of an effective CRM system manifests in various ways, making it an invaluable tool for any business. Firstly, it enhances efficiency. An effective CRM system acts as a conduit, systematically consolidating customer data into one central location, making it easily accessible for employees across all levels of the corporate ladder. This ultimately saves time and enhances productivity (Olsen & Danielle, 2018).

Secondly, an efficient CRM system increases profitability. It provides profound insights into customer behavior, enabling businesses to create targeted marketing strategies. By harnessing the integrated analytics provided by CRM, businesses can identify the most profitable customer groups, thus maximizing ROI (Ngai, Xiu & Chau, 2009).

Effective CRM implementation is crucial, and it involves several key considerations. Planning is a key stage to set the right expectations. Here, businesses should extensively define their goals and aims. Additionally, the entire company needs to understand the reason behind the new system for it to succeed. Secondly, businesses should ensure that the CRM software chosen aligns with their business model and processes. It should be user-friendly to encourage end-user adoption, and robust enough to accommodate future growth (Trainor et al., 2014).

Moreover, data migration is an important aspect of CRM implementation. Companies should scrutinize all data and migrate only what's relevant, ensuring it is clean and reliable. Training is another critical component that influences successful CRM implementation. Every end-user must become proficient in the software to fully exploit its potential.

Ongoing support and post-implementation evaluations are essential for maintaining CRM system effectiveness. They help identify potential issues before they escalate, thus promoting optimal utilization of the system (Trainor et al., 2014).

In conclusion, an effective CRM system is an invaluable tool for modern businesses. It consolidates customer data, and provides customer insight, thus allowing for personalized strategies, leading to increased customer engagement and profitability. While the importance of a CRM system cannot be understated, businesses must appreciate that its successful implementation requires careful planning, the right software selection, effective training, and ongoing support. These combined elements will guarantee the unleashing of the true potential of a CRM system, thus catalyzing growth and sustained competitive advantage.

RESOURCES AND FURTHER READING

List of useful resources and links for further reading on CRM.

Lauded as a powerful tool that streamlines business operations and enhances customer relationships, Customer Relationship Management (CRM) has become an integral aspect of modern business strategy. If you are interested in diving deeper into the world of CRM, here are a selection of resources and links to enhance your understanding and knowledge base.

1. Salesforce Blog (https://www.salesforce.com/blog/): As the leading provider of CRM solutions, Salesforce offers a robust blog full of invaluable insights, tips, and trends on CRM. The articles are infused with expert knowledge and practical tips that can help businesses optimally utilize CRM systems.

2. Zoho Blog (https://www.zoho.com/blog/): Zoho's blog provides a wealth of information on CRM, tackling varied aspects like CRM implementation, features, analytics, and integration with other software. It's especially useful for small to medium-sized businesses looking to make the most out of their CRM systems.

3. Microsoft Dynamics CRM Blog (https://community.dynamics.com/crm/b/crmconnectio

n): Managed by the Microsoft Dynamics Community, this blog contains a plethora of information on CRM and its practice — particularly for users of Microsoft Dynamics CRM. Topics covered range from software updates to innovative CRM strategies.

4. CRM Buyer (https://www.crmbuyer.com/): As its name suggests, CRM Buyer is a dedicated hub for CRM-related content. They offer a wide range of articles, news, and blogs on CRM strategy and usage, making it a great resource for CRM enthusiasts and professionals alike.

5. CRM Base (https://www.crm.com/blog): CRM Base focuses on providing invaluable CRM content to readers. The blog offers a mix of CRM-related news, tips, trends, and guides.

6.   Forbes   -   CRM (https://www.forbes.com/crm/#7dfe0d814927): Forbes offers a plethora of resources on current CRM topics, trends, and best practices. Their articles range from thought leadership pieces on CRM strategy to reviews of different CRM solutions.

7.   Software   Advice (https://www.softwareadvice.com/crm/): If you're interested in CRM software reviews, including comparison charts and detailed features, Software Advice is an indispensable resource.

8. Gartner (https://www.gartner.com/en): Gartner provides insightful research, analysis, and advice on CRM, particularly regarding technology and its impact on businesses.

9. Book - CRM at the Speed of Light by Paul Greenberg: This book is considered a must-read on the subject of CRM. Greenberg dives into the social and technical

aspects of CRM, offering comprehensive insights into its implementation and benefits.

10. Book - The CRM Handbook by Jill Dyche: As an insightful guide to understanding and implementing CRM, this book provides practical advice, case studies, and strategies.

These resources provide a wealth of knowledge and can undoubtedly elevate your comprehension of CRM. Continually educating oneself is crucial in a field like CRM, where technology is rapidly evolving.

Table of contents

A. Role of management in successful CRM adoption

B. Training staff for CRM implementation

C. Regularly updating and cleaning up your CRM system

D. Monitoring and evaluation of CRM practices

VI. INTEGRATING CRM WITH OTHER BUSINESS SYSTEMS

A. The role of CRM in sales and marketing campaigns

B. Integrating CRM with HR, finance, and other business software

C. Using CRM for business analytics.

VII. CASE STUDIES OF SUCCESSFUL CRM IMPLEMENTATION

A. Industry-specific case studies highlighting the successful use of CRM

B. Lessons learned – what worked and what did not?

C. Relevance of the case study to your business

VIII. CHALLENGES AND PITFALLS IN ADOPTING CRM

A. Common mistakes businesses make when adopting a CRM system

B. How to overcome these challenges and pitfalls

C. The future of CRM – upcoming trends and innovations

IX. CONCLUSION

A. Recap of key points discussed in the eBook

B. Final thoughts on the importance and implementation of an effective CRM system for businesses

X. RESOURCES AND FURTHER READING

A. List of useful resources and links for further reading on CRM.

9 789358 830972